WELCOME!

This book belongs to

....

Aged ....

Before we begin, remember...
whenever we read or hear the name of Allah, we say:
Subhaana huwa taala

Whenever we read or hear the name of Muhammad (s), we say:
Salalahu alayhi wasalam

Whenever we read or hear the name of other prophets, we say:
Alayhi salaam

What is... RAMADHAN?

Ramadhan is the ninth month of the Islamic calendar. The exact dates change every year because Islam uses a calendar based on the cycles of the Moon.

During Ramadhan, Muslims will not eat or drink during the hours of daylight. This is called fasting or sawm in Arabic. Children do not have to fast until they are old enough, which is usually around the age of 14. Women who are having babies, old people, ill people and travellers also do not need to fast.

Ramadhan also marks the month in which the Quran was first revealed to the Prophet Muhammad (s). The night that it was revealed is known as Laylat-ul Qadr or The Night of Power.

During Ramadhan, it is common to have one meal known as the suhoor, just before dawn and another known as the iftar after sunset.

Almost all Muslims try to give up bad habits during Ramadhan. It is a time for prayer and good deeds. Many will attempt to read the whole of the Quran at least once during Ramadhan, and some people go to special prayers in the Mosque called Taraweeh.

When Ramadhan is over, Muslims celebrate on a day called Eid ul Fitr, the Festival of the Breaking of the Fast.

Muslims often talk about Ramadhan as a guest that visits their home once a year for just one month.

Use the page opposite to write a letter welcoming Ramadhan. Think about the things you might be looking forward to and what you might find difficult.

Dear Ramadhan,

WORDSEARCH

Can you find the ten Ramadhan words hidden in the puzzle? Tick them off the list below once you find each name!

T	P	D	H	I	K	R	O	D	U
A	R	F	U	A	Q	U	R	A	N
R	H	A	J	L	W	E	A	T	E
A	U	S	M	O	S	Q	U	E	C
W	Y	T	D	A	T	X	M	S	N
E	L	I	S	H	D	I	O	C	E
E	O	N	V	C	A	H	D	V	I
H	E	G	Z	I	E	U	A	G	T
S	T	R	E	N	G	T	H	N	A
R	T	I	F	L	U	D	I	E	P

RAMADHAN
FASTING
DATES
MOSQUE
QURAN

TARAWEEH
PATIENCE
STRENGTH
DHIKR
EID UL FITR

The first REVELATION

When the Prophet Muhammad (s) was forty years old he would often go away for a few days to the mountains near Makkah and spend time alone. He would think about the world around him. His wife, Khadija would prepare some food for the few days he was away.

One night, the Prophet was in a cave called Hira, near the outskirts of Makkah. Allah sent the angel Jibrael in the form of a man, to visit Muhammad (s).

Jibrael commanded the Prophet "Iqra" which means read! The angel squeezed the Prophet very hard and again commanded "Iqra". The angel squeezed him very hard a second time and commanded him "Iqra".

The angel squeezed the Prophet for a third time and this time recited five verses. These were the first verses of the Holy Quran to be revealed. The Prophet finally repeated the words.

After this, the Prophet ran home and told his wife and they went to see Waraqah, a learned man, who confirmed that this was an angel that had brought a divine message to Muhammad (s).

The Prophet continued to get verses from Allah over the next twenty-three years. These verses are the Quran which we have with us today.

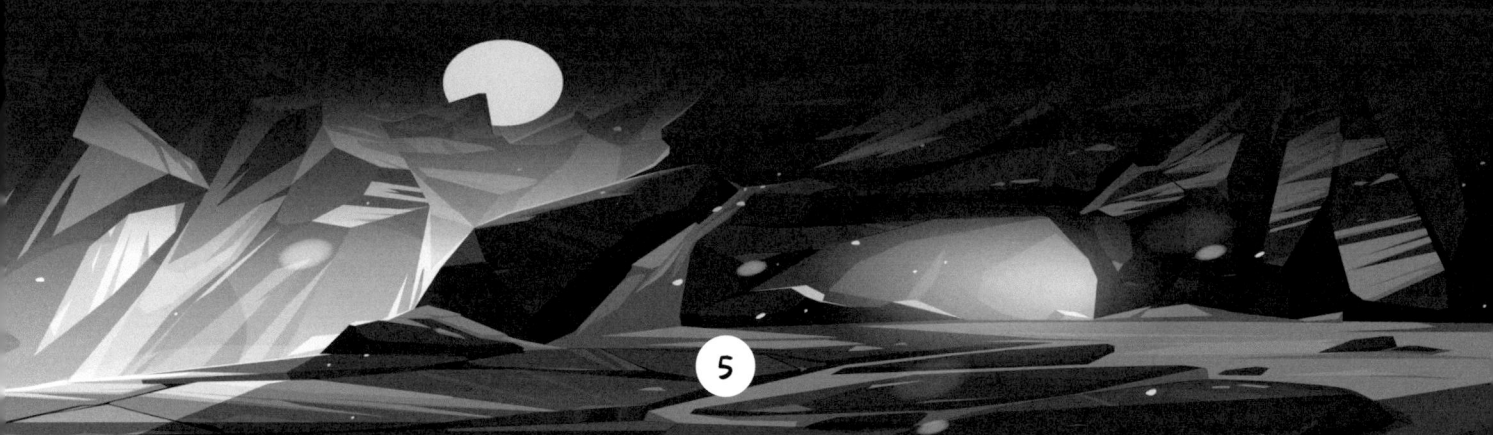

WHAT TIME IS IT?

Knowing what time it is, is very important when we are fasting.

We need to know what time the fast begins, this is SUHOOR.

We need to know what time the fast ends, this is IFTAR.

We also need to know the time of the prayers so that we can offer our salah on time. The most important prayer times when fasting are the morning prayer, or FAJR and the sunset prayer, or MAGHRIB.

Draw the hands on each of the clocks below to show the correct timings for tomorrow's fast.

SUHOOR

FAJR

IFTAR

MAGHRIB

WRITING ABOUT RAMADHAN

Look at the pictures and words below. Try to write a few sentences about each picture using some or all of the words in the list. Think about what the pictures mean to you and how they make you feel when you experience them. Use a separate sheet of paper if you need more space.

RESPECT
ALLAH
WORSHIP
MEET
PRAY
LISTEN

READ
LEARN
ARABIC
WISDOM
HOLY
RECITE

QIBLA
PRAY
SUJOOD
TIME
THINK
WUDHU

QUESTION TIME!

Let's see what you have learnt so far with a quick quiz to test your knowledge!

Draw a line from each of the questions on the left to the correct answer on the right.

WHAT MONTH OF THE ISLAMIC CALENDAR IS RAMADHAN?	SUHOOR AND IFTAAR
WHAT IS THE NAME FOR THE NIGHT ON WHICH THE QURAN WAS REVEALED?	LAYLAT-UL QADR OR THE NIGHT OF POWER
ISLAM USES A CALENDAR BASED ON WHAT?	DURING DAYLIGHT HOURS
WHAT ARE THE NAMES OF THE TWO MEALS?	NINTH
WHO VISITED THE PROPHET WITH THE REVELATION?	THE CYCLES OF THE MOON
WHEN IN RAMADHAN DO MUSLIMS NOT EAT OR DRINK ANYTHING?	THE ANGEL JIBRAEL

COLOUR US IN!

VIRTUES OF

During the holy month of Ramadhan, the doors of paradise are opened. The doors of hell are locked and the devils are all chained up.

Every night of Ramadhan, Allah sets free many thousands of people from the fire of hell.

The first part of the month is linked to mercy, the second part to forgiveness and the third part to salvation (safety from hell.)

Every good deed you do in Ramadhan, the reward is multiplied. Allah says one deed is multiplied between 10 and 700 times, except for fasting because this is for Him alone, and He will give the reward Himself.

RAMADHAN!

The smell from the mouth of a fasting person is more fragrant in the eyes of Allah than the smell of perfume.

When you perform a Nafl (extra) act in Ramadhan you are rewarded with that of a fardh (necessary). When you perform a Fardh act, it is multiplied 70 times.

Whoever gives food to a fasting person to break the fast, his sins will be forgiven and he will be saved from the fire. Even if it is a sip of water, milk or a date.

Whoever feeds a fasting person, Allah will give him water from the Hawz-e-kawthar. Whoever drinks from this water will never feel thirsty until he enters paradise.

THE WAY HOME!

Can you help me get home before Iftar?

Lead me through the maze till you get me back home in the centre!

Avoid the walls blocking our way, or you will have to start all over again!

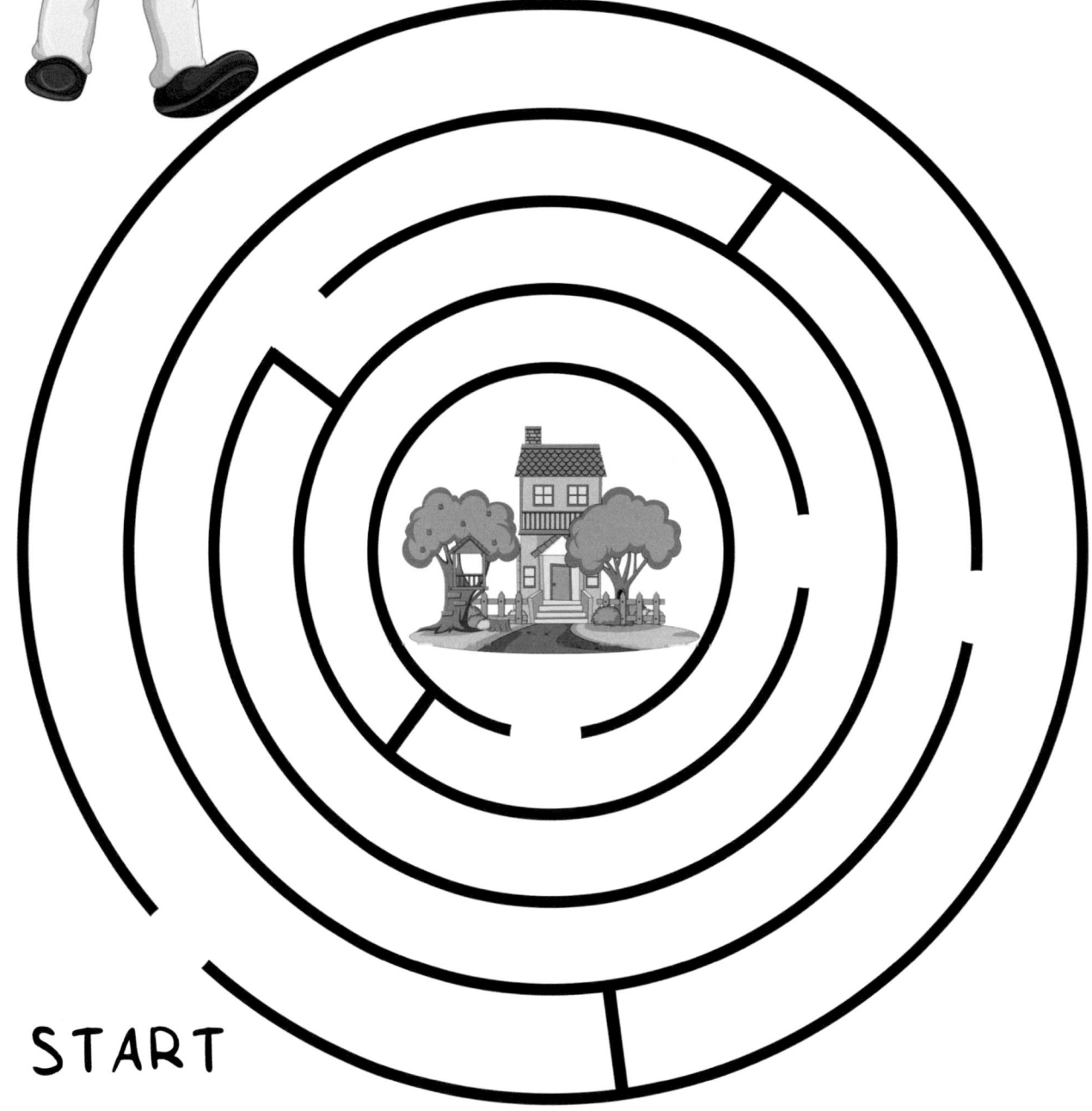

START

CROSSWORD

Can you answer all of the clues below and write their answers in the correct box?

ACROSS
3. The prayers offered in the mosque each night of Ramadhan.
4. The ninth month of the Islamic calendar.
7. What is the second part of the month linked to.

DOWN
1. The age when Prophet Muhammad (s) got the first revelation.
2. What is the third part of the month linked to.
5. The mountain where the first revelation was revealed.
6. What is the first part of the month linked to.
8. The Arabic word for fasting.

MOSQUE MANNERS!

During the month of Ramadhan, you might find yourself at the mosque more often than normal.

You might attend taraweeh prayers in the evenings. You might go to listen to special speeches. Or you might go to help with charity work Insha Allah.

Whatever you go for, you should always remember that when you are in the mosque you should be on your best behaviour and display your best manners.

You should be an example for others in the mosque and remember that you are in a House of Allah.

See if you can fill in the sentences on the opposite page with the words listed at the bottom. But remember, you can only use each word once!

MY PROMISE TO THE MOSQUE

When I go to the _____ I will always be on my very best _____ .

I will not be _____ and I most certainly will not _____.

When I enter the mosque, I will enter with my right _____ first.

I will be _____ and say _____ to the people I meet.

If it is time for _____ , I will be _____.

If there is a _____ going on I will make sure that I quietly _____ .

The mosque is a special place.

It is a _____ of _____ .

HOUSE	PRAYERS	FOOT	MOSQUE	ALLAH
BEHAVIOUR	QUIET	MISBEHAVE		ASALAM ALEYKUM
NAUGHTY	SERMON	POLITE	LISTEN

DOT 2 DOT

During the month of Ramadhan, many people hang up twinkling lights or lanterns filled with candles around their home. This is a beautiful way of celebrating the blessings of the month!

Connect the dots from numbers 1 to 20 to complete the lantern.

CAN YOU LEARN YOUR DUA?

It is really important that you know the correct dua to read when you begin your fasting and when you end it. This is a dua you will be reading every day, so it should be easy for you to try and memorise!

THE DUA TO BEGIN YOUR FAST AT SUHOOR TIME IS...

وَبِصَوْمِ غَدٍ نَّوَيْتُ مِنْ شَهْرِ رَمَضَانَ

Wa bisawmi ghadinn nawaiytu min shahri Ramadan

which means...
I intend to keep the fast tomorrow in the month of Ramadhan.

THE DUA TO END YOUR FAST AT IFTAR TIME IS...

اللَّهُمَّ اِنِّى لَكَ صُمْتُ وَبِكَ امنْتُ وَعَلَيْكَ تَوَكَّلتُ وَ عَلى رِزْقِكَ اَفْطَرْتُ

Allahumma inni laka sumtu
wa bika aamantu
wa alayka tawakkaltu
wa ala rizq-ika-aftartu

which means...
O Allah, I fasted for You,
and I believe in You,
and I put my trust in you,
and I break my fast with Your sustenance.

See if you can learn these duas by heart. It might be hard at first, but keep trying and you will get there in no time at all!

UNSCRAMBLE THE LETTERS!

Can you rearrange the letters on the left to discover the hidden Ramadhan related words? Write your answers in the spaces on the right!

AWMS = _____

ARATWEHE = _____

HANDARMA = _____

ESOQUM = _____

TRIFA = _____

NAQRU = _____

OROSHU = _____

KIDRH = _____

LAYLAT-UL QADR
THE NIGHT THE QURAN WAS REVEALED

Laylat-ul Qadr is the Night of Power. Allah says in the Quran that it is better than a thousand months. This means worshipping Allah on that night is better than worshipping Him for a thousand months. So any extra worship you do has more reward on Laylat-ul Qadr than on any other night of the year.

Extra worship can include reciting extra dhikr or reading and understanding Quran and Tafseer. You could do Itikaaf, this is where you stay in the mosque for a certain number of days and devote yourself to worship. Making dua to Allah is also extra worship, to praise Him, ask for forgiveness, His help and blessings.

When the Prophet of Allah was asked what night Laylat-ul Qadr was, he said it was an odd night, in the last portion of the month of Ramadhan. Most people believe it to be on the 27th night of Ramadhan, but the exact night is a secret only Allah knows!

Think about what you will do for extra worship on the night of Laylat-ul Qadr and write it down below.

ON LAYLAT-UL QADR I WILL...

_____
_____
_____
_____
_____

FASTING IS FUN!

Fasting is one of the 5 pillars of Islam.

In fact, it is the fourth pillar.

During the special month of Ramadhan, Muslims stop eating and drinking from dawn until sunset. We keep this fast to gain lots of reward and blessings from Allah Most High.

When a person is fasting, they not only stop eating and drinking but they also do lots of good deeds such as: being kind, giving to charity, praying more and trying to not to sin.

Fasting in this month may last for 29 or 30 days depending on when the new moon is sighted. This marks the day of Eid, when Muslims celebrate and do not need to fast any longer.

ASK ALLAH

Dua is asking Allah directly for what we want. We do this because not only is Allah the only one worthy of our duas, but it also pleases Him when we turn to Him.

We can ask Allah for anything, but He will only give it to us if it is good for us, and the dua made at the time of Iftar is not rejected!

Make a list of what you will make dua for during the month of Ramadhan. Think of what will make you happy, but also what will please Allah.

MY RAMADHAN DUA LIST

WHAT ARE...

Taraweeh are special prayers that Muslims pray in the holy month of Ramadhan. They are slightly longer than the usual night prayer that is read outside of Ramadhan.

It consists of 20 units of prayer and can be read in cycles of 2 or 4 units. After the fourth cycle of units, there is a special dua that is recited.

TARAWEEH?

This prayer is Sunnah, as our beloved Prophet would pray it, and many times he would pray it in congregation in the Masjid but sometimes he read it alone at home. It is prayed at night with the Isha prayer before Fajr time.

Different parts of the Quran are read in this prayer. In fact, many Imams will choose to complete a full Quran during the Taraweeh prayer and earn immense reward and blessings.

RAMADHAN

Ramadhan is the perfect time to do good deeds. Remember, the reward you will receive can be multiplied by Allah during this time!

Use the calendar below and each day, write down the good deeds you do! By the end of Ramadhan you will be able to add up all of your deeds and calculate your total for the month!

1	2	3
4	5	6
7	8	9
10	11	12
13	14	15

GOOD DEEDS

TARGET
I want to try to complete this many good deeds during the month of Ramadhan

TOTAL
I managed to complete this many good deeds during the month of Ramadhan

16	17	18
19	20	21
22	23	24
25	26	27
28	29	30

TRUE OR FALSE

Now that we have read and understood all of the information about the month of Ramadhan, can you tell which of the statements below are true and which are false? Take a pen and draw a circle around the correct answers.

1. FASTING MEANS NO EATING OR DRINKING DURING DAYLIGHT HOURS   TRUE   FALSE

2. SINS, LIKE LYING, CHEATING AND SWEARING ARE ALLOWED IN THE MONTH OF RAMADHAN   TRUE   FALSE

3. MY FAST IS BROKEN IF I EAT OR DRINK DURING DAYLIGHT HOURS   TRUE   FALSE

4. IF I FORGETFULLY OR ACCIDENTALLY EAT DURING MY FAST, IT IS NOT BROKEN. ALLAH FORGIVES US!   TRUE   FALSE

5. EVERYBODY MUST FAST! EVEN IF YOU ARE SICK, TOO OLD, TOO YOUNG OR TRAVELLING   TRUE   FALSE

6. ISLAMIC MONTHS LIKE RAMADHAN ARE BASED ON THE CYCLES OF THE MOON	TRUE	FALSE
7. RAMADHAN HAS A SET NUMBER OF 30 DAYS	TRUE	FALSE
8. IN RAMADHAN DEVILS ARE FREE TO ROAM AND ENCOURAGE US TO EAT!	TRUE	FALSE
9. FASTING GIVES US TAQWA AND MAKES US BETTER, MORE PIOUS MUSLIMS	TRUE	FALSE
10. FASTING IS THE FIRST PILLAR OF ISLAM	TRUE	FALSE
11. TARAWEEH PRAYERS CAN BE PRAYED DURING THE AFTERNOON	TRUE	FALSE
12. ALLAH SAYS IN THE QURAN THAT THE NIGHT OF LAYLAT-UL QADR IS BETTER THAN A THOUSAND MONTHS	TRUE	FALSE

EID! EID! EID!

The day after our last fast, when Ramadhan has ended, is Eid ul Fitr. This is the big celebration where people pray at the mosque, meet with their families, enjoy delicious food and have fun!

Fold an A4 sheet of paper in half to make a card. Now decorate it and write it out to a friend or family member to show them how much you care!

You can use some of the designs or pictures below to give you some ideas. Copy them out to make your card look really amazing!

SAYING GOODBYE TO THE HOLY MONTH

Just like at the start of this book, you wrote a letter welcoming Ramadhan, now write a letter saying goodbye. Think about the things you enjoyed most about Ramadhan this year. Think about the good habits you have learnt and how you might keep them up throughout the rest of the year.

Dear Ramadhan,

ACTIVITY ANSWERS

WORDSEARCH

QUESTION TIME

WHAT MONTH OF THE ISLAMIC CALENDAR IS RAMADHAN? NINTH

WHAT IS THE NAME FOR THE NIGHT ON WHICH THE QURAN WAS REVEALED? LAYLUT AL QADR OR THE NIGHT OF POWER

ISLAM USES A CALENDAR BASED ON WHAT? THE CYCLES OF THE MOON

WHAT ARE THE NAMES OF THE TWO MEALS? SUHOOR AND IFTAAR

WHO VISITED THE PROPHET WITH THE REVELATION? THE ANGEL JIBRAEL

WHEN IN RAMADHAN DO MUSLIMS NOT EAT OR DRINK ANYTHING? DURING DAYLIGHT HOURS

THE WAY HOME!

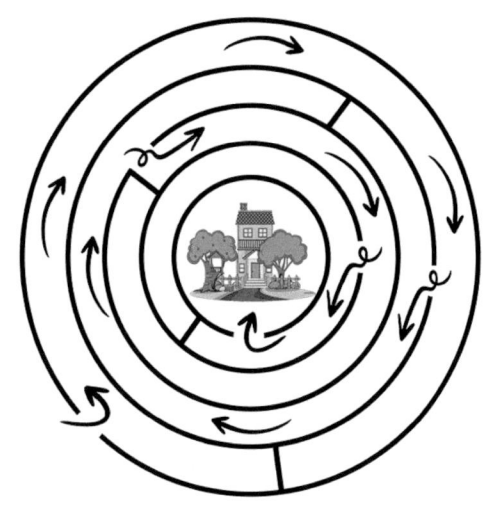

CROSSWORD

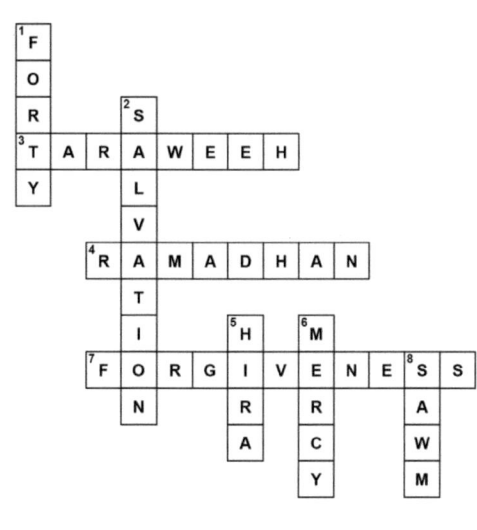

DOT2DOT

MY PROMISE TO THE MOSQUE

When I go to the MOSQUE I will always be on my very best BEHAVIOUR. I will not be NAUGHTY and I most certainly will not MISBEHAVE. When I enter the mosque, I will enter with my right FOOT first. I will be POLITE and say ASALAM ALEYKUM to the people I meet. If it is time for PRAYERS I will be QUIET. If there is a SERMON going on I will make sure that I quietly LISTEN. The mosque is a special place. It is a HOUSE of ALLAH.

UNSCRAMBLE THE LETTERS
SAWM, TARAWEEH, RAMADHAN, MOSQUE, IFTAR, QURAN, SUHOOR, DHIKR

TRUE OR FALSE
1. T 2. F 3. T 4. T 5. F 6. T 7. F 8. F 9. T 10. F 11. F 12. T

Printed by Libri Plureos GmbH in Hamburg, Germany